To my friend, Marco Lo Muscio

Variations on "Greensleeves"
(What Child Is This)

Sw. Reeds 8'
Gt. Full organ with Reeds, Sw. to Gt.
Ch. Full organ with Reeds, Sw. to Ch.
Ped. Full organ with Reeds

Traditional English Melody
Arr. by GRIMOALDO MACCHIA (b. 1972)

1. Entrée

Allegro e declamato

12
Sw.
fff
18
Ch.
ff
22
5
26
Gt.
fff

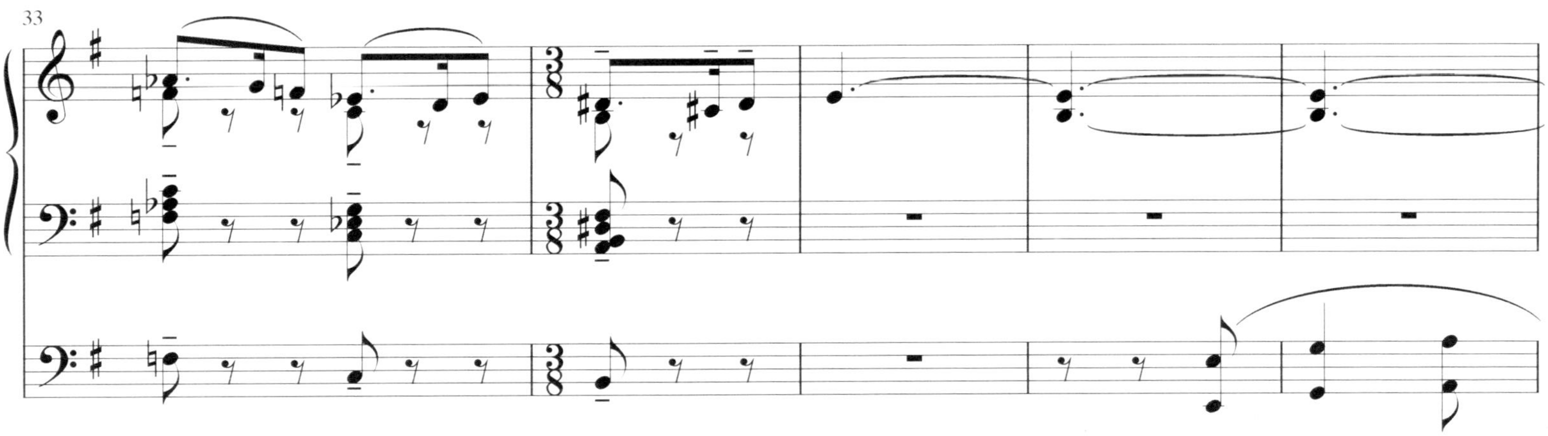

Sw. Vox Celeste
Gt. Cornet
Ch. Bourdon 8' (2')
Ped. Subbass 16'

2. Mistic Adagios

Meditativo

Sw.
p
Sw.
Ch.
p

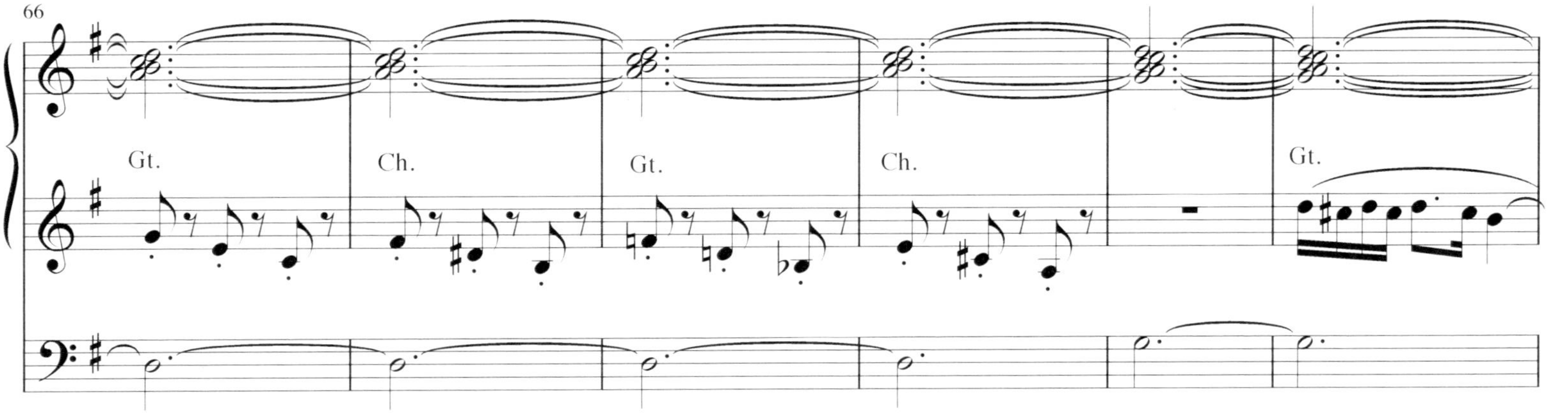

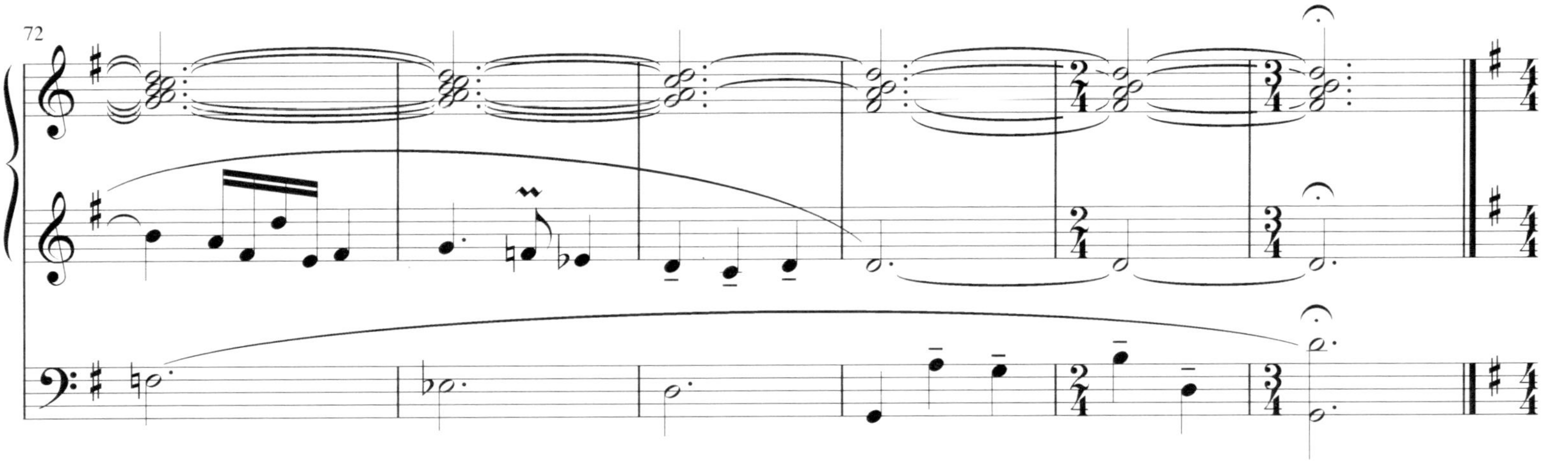

Sw. Reeds 8', Sw. to Gt.
Gt. Foundations 8', 4', Reeds, Gt. to Ch.
Ch. Foundations 8', 4', Reeds, Sw. to Ch.
Ped. Foundations 16', 8', Reeds 16', 8'

3. Royal Fanfare

Festosa

fff

4. Scherzo

Sw. Bourdon 8' (2')
Ch. Harmonic Flute 8'

Vivace e leggero

5. Festive March

Sw. Foundations 8', 4', Reeds 8'
Gt. Foundations 8', 4', 2', Mixt., Sw. to Gt.
Ch. Foundations 8', 4', 2', Mixt., Ch to Gt.
Ped. Foundations 16', 8', Sw. to Ped.

Cantabile
132
Sw.
mp
p
134
1
136
2
Ch.
f
138
3

Gt. Foundations 8', 4', 2',
Mixt., Sw. to Gt.

Gt. Foundations 8', 4', 2', Mixt., Reeds, Gt. to Ped.
Ped. Foundations 16,' 8', 4', Reeds

6. Pedal Solo

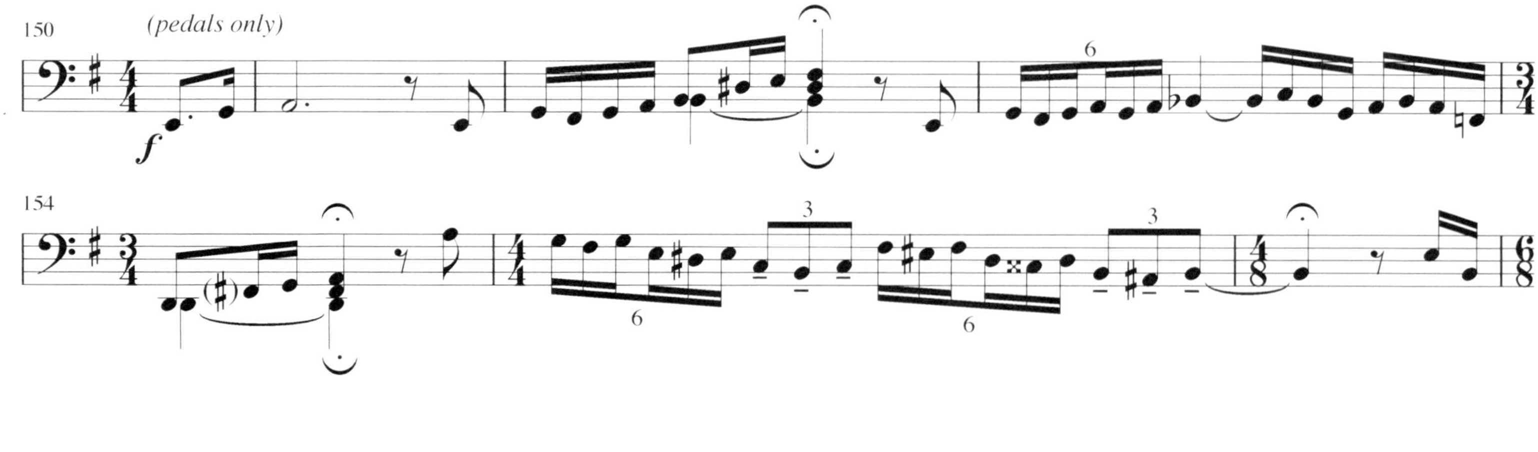

Risolutivo
Gt.
ff

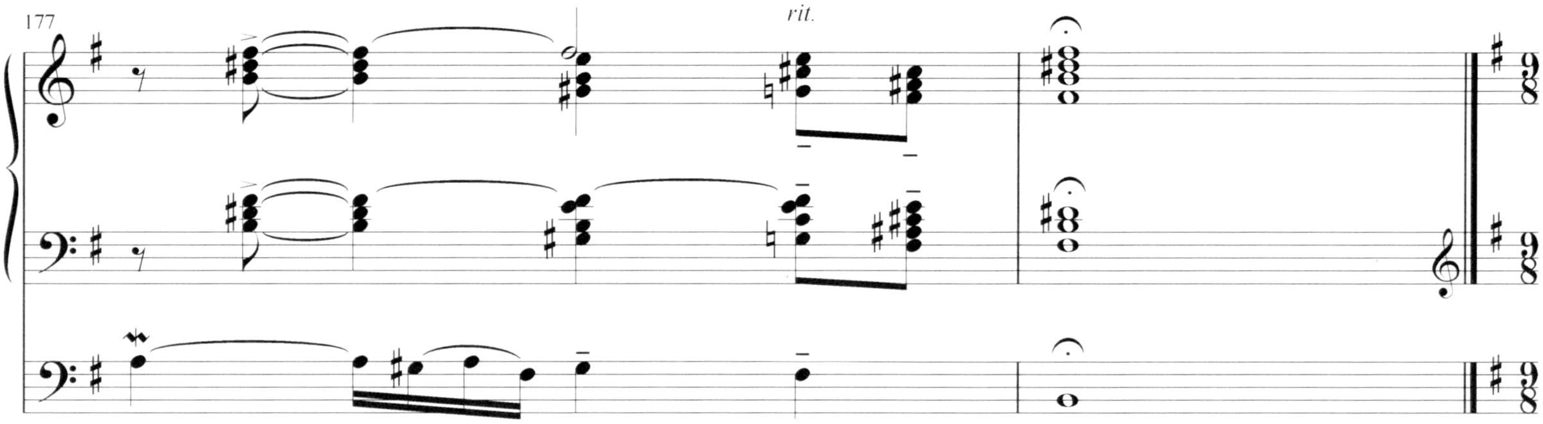

Sw. Foundations 8', 4', Reeds 8'
Gt. Foundations 8', 4', 2', Sw. to Gt.
Ch. Foundations 8', 4', 2', Gt. to Ch.
Ped. Foundations 16', 8', Sw. to Ped.

7. Little Toccatas

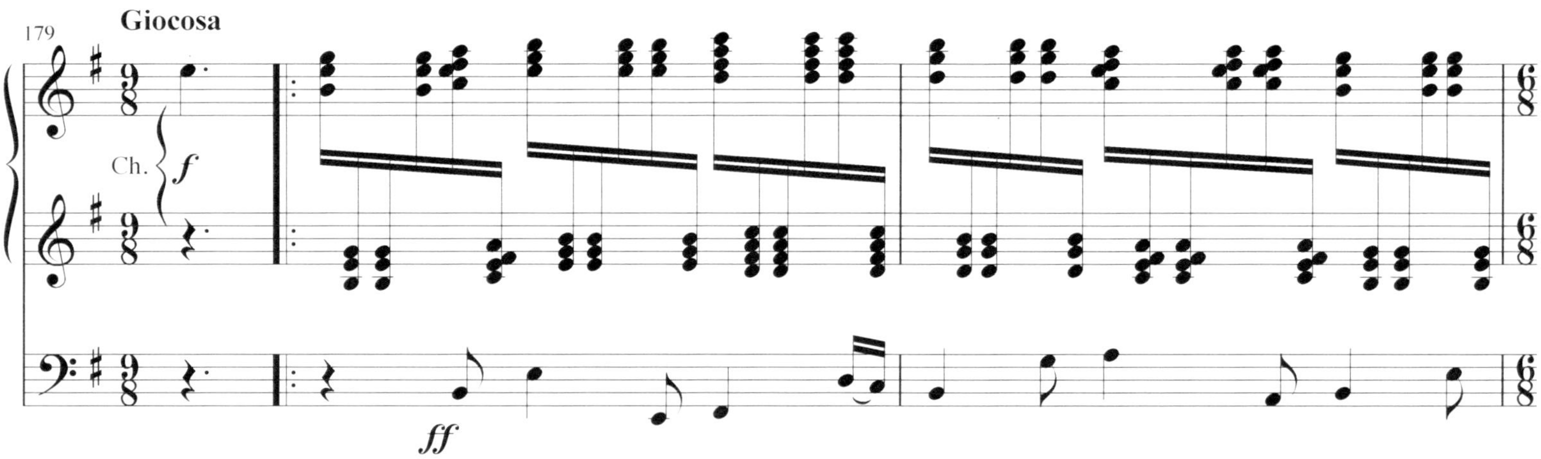

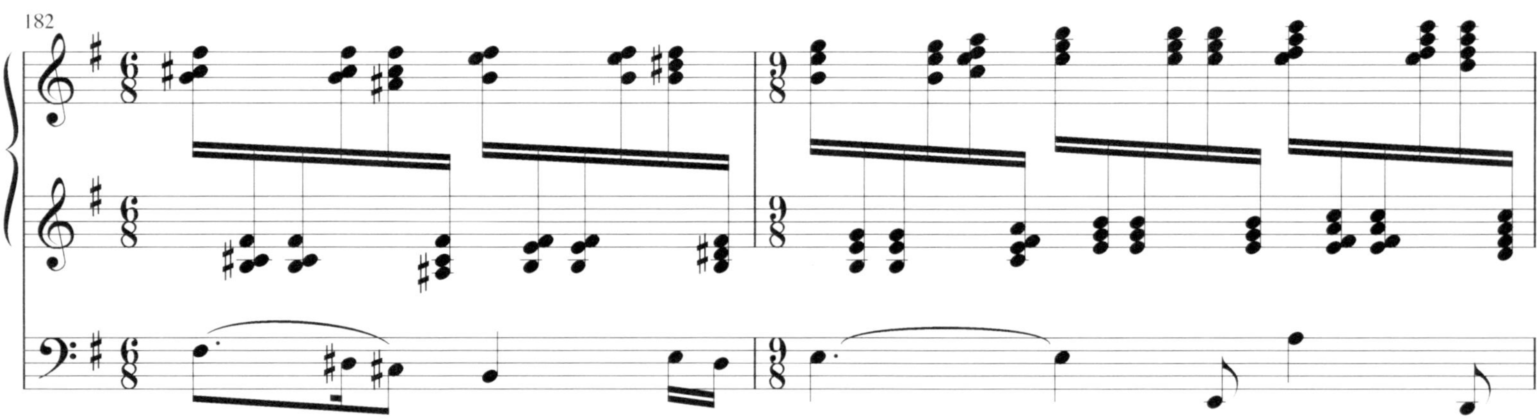

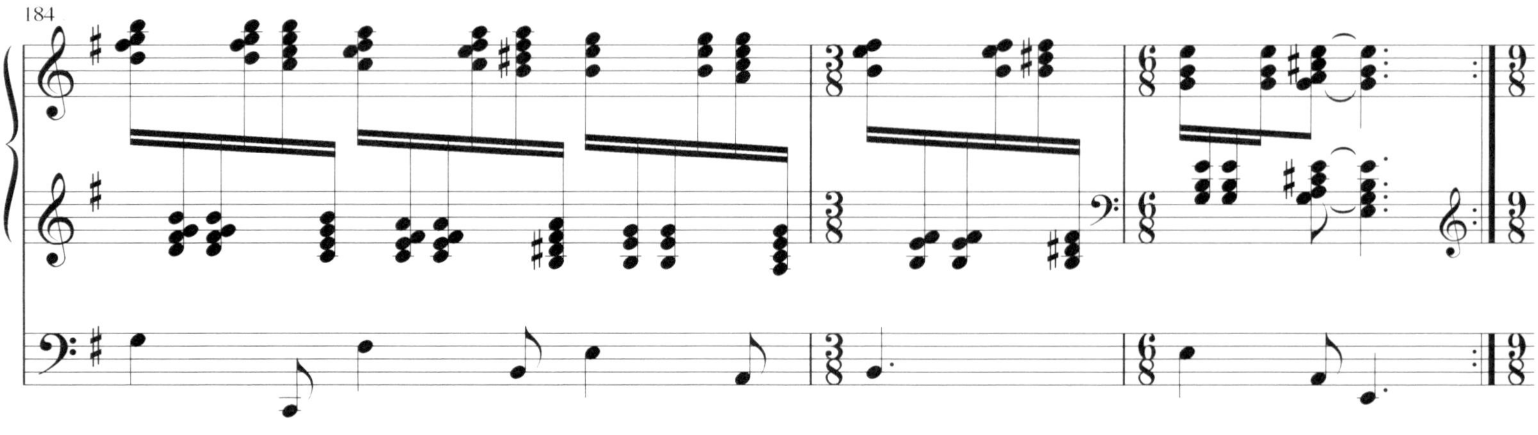

187
189
191
(cadenza)
193
9
ff

8. Trio – Choral

Sw. Foundations 8'
Gt. Cornet
Ped. Foundations 16', 8'

Sw. Foundations 8', 4', Reeds 8'
Gt. Foundations 8', 4', 2', Mixt., Reeds 8', Sw. to Gt.
Ch. Foundations 8', 4', 2'
Ped. Foundations 16', 8' (with Reeds 8')

9. Fuga

219
223
mf
227
f
231

235
239
243
Gt.
247
ff
12

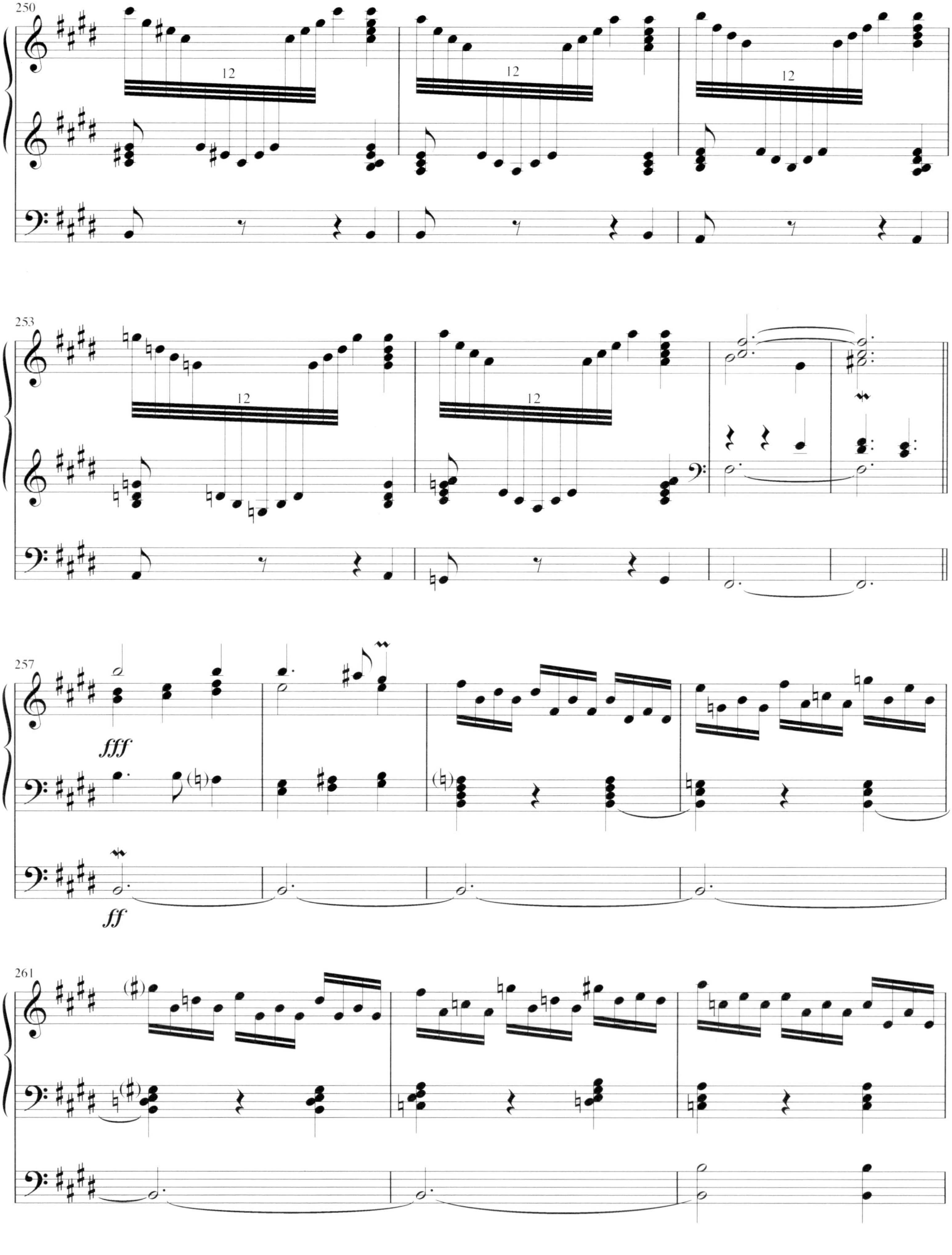
250
12
12
12
253
12
12
257
fff
ff
261
(♯)
(♮)
(♯)

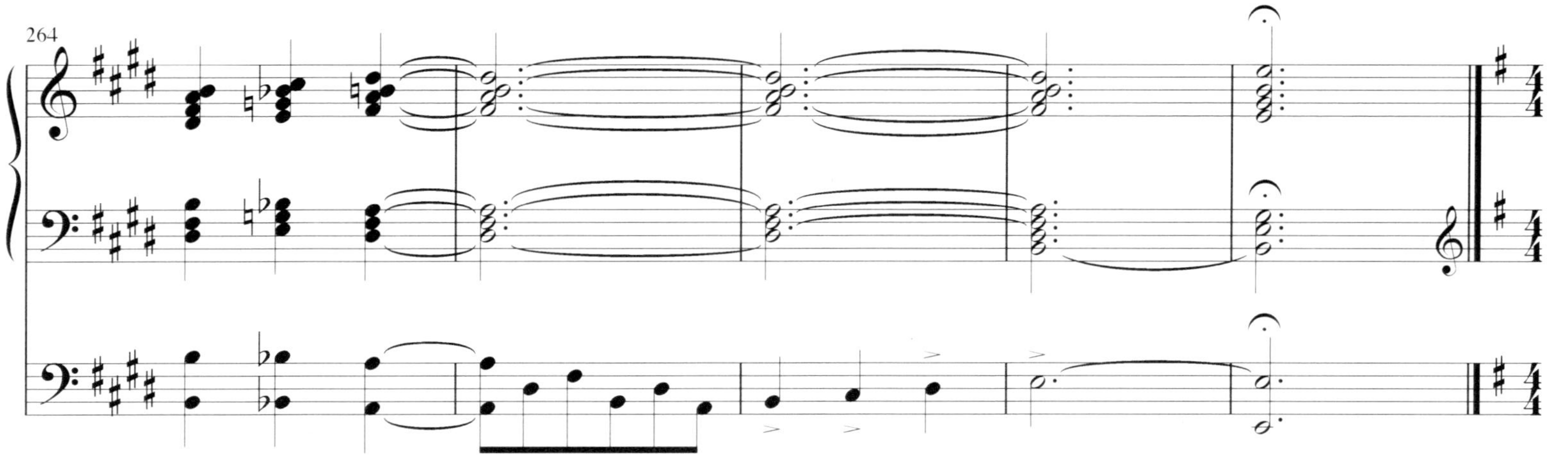

Sw. Foundations 8', 4', Reeds 8'
Gt. Foundations 8', 4', 2', Mixt., Reeds 8', Sw. to Gt.
Ch. Foundations 8', 4', 2'
Ped. Foundations 16', 8', Reeds 8'

10. Progressiv Rock

279
282
284
288

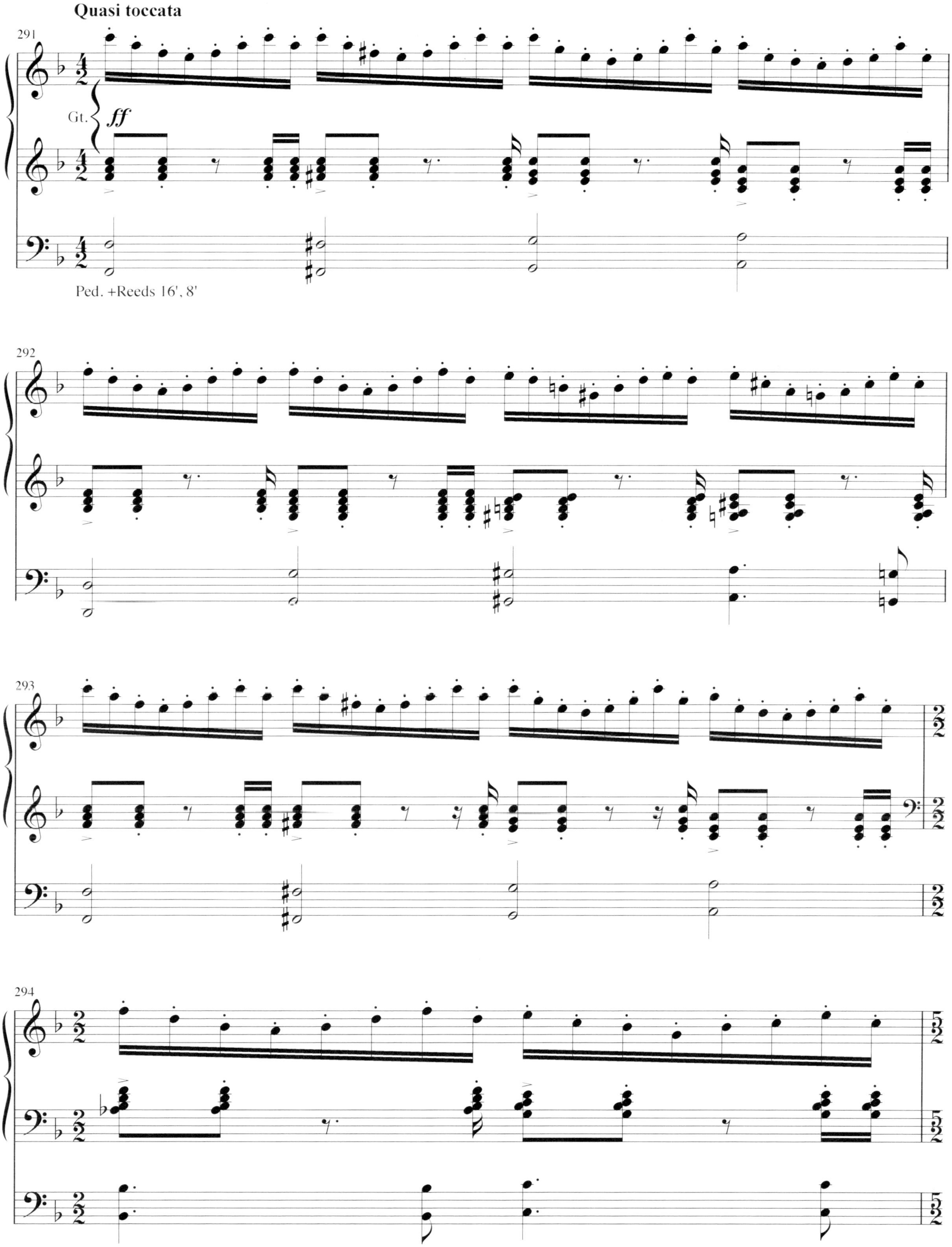
Quasi toccata
291
Gt.
ff
Ped. +Reeds 16', 8'
292
293
294

Sw. Foundations 8', 4'
Gt. Foundations 8', 4', Reeds 8', 4'
Ch. Foundations 8', 4'
Ped. Foundations 16', 8'
Manuals coupled

11. Sortié – Carillon

Andante con moto

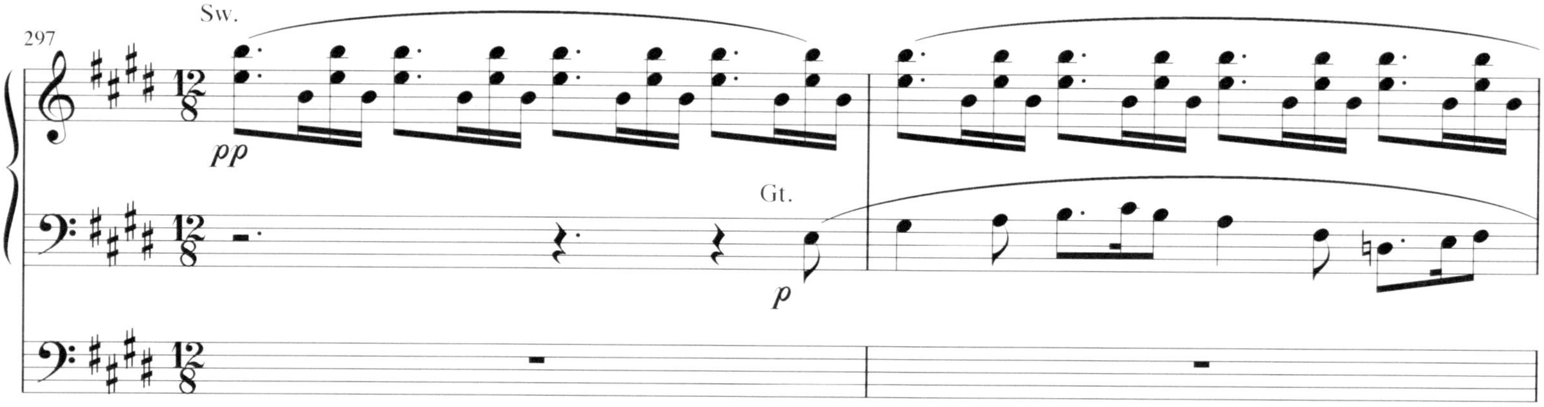

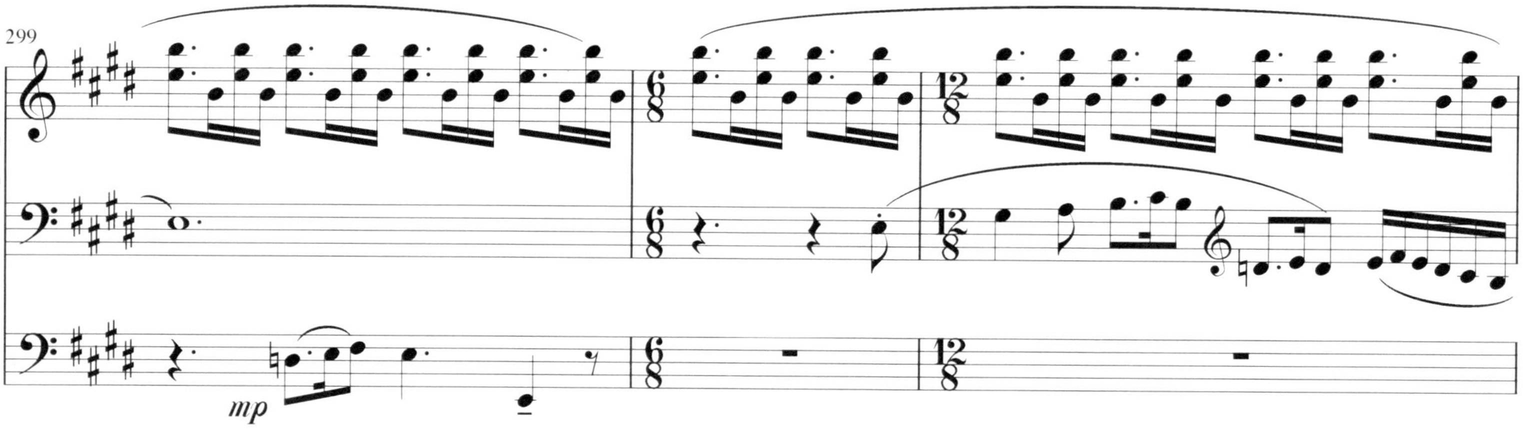

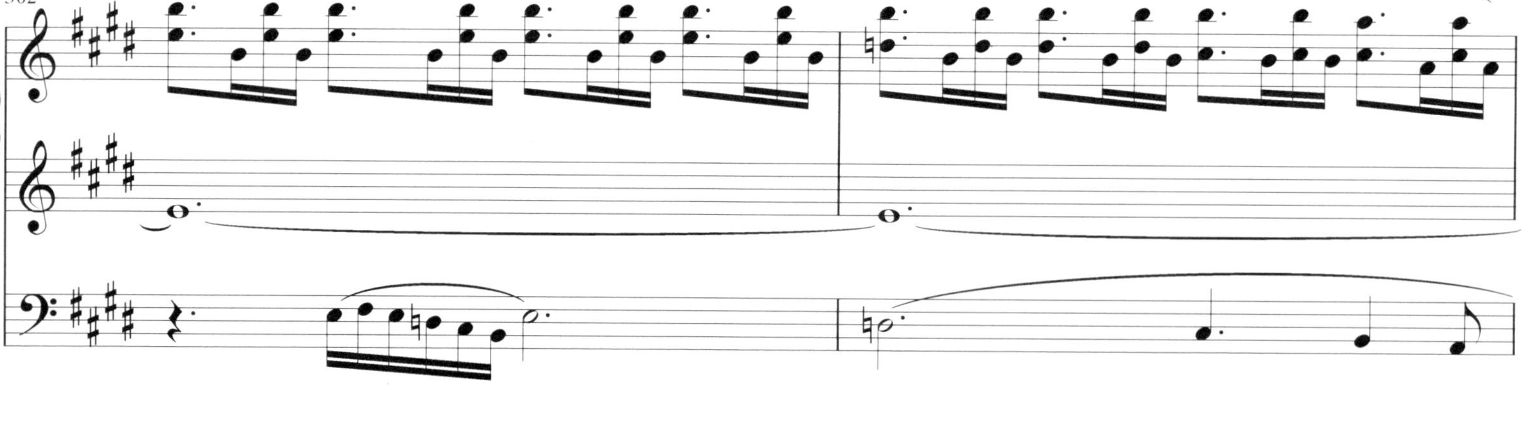

304
306
308
310

312
f
ff
314
f
317
319

321
323
Sw.
Ch.
Ped. +Foundation 32'
325
327
Sw.

329
331
Ch.
mp
Gt. Solo (Cromorno/Regale)
mf
p
333
335

Sw. Foundations 8', 4', Reeds 8', 4'
Gt. Foundations 8', 4', Reeds 16', 8', 4'
Ch. Foundations 8', 4', Reeds 16', 8', 4'
Ped. Foundations 32', 16', 8', Reeds 32', 16', 8', 4'
Manuals coupled

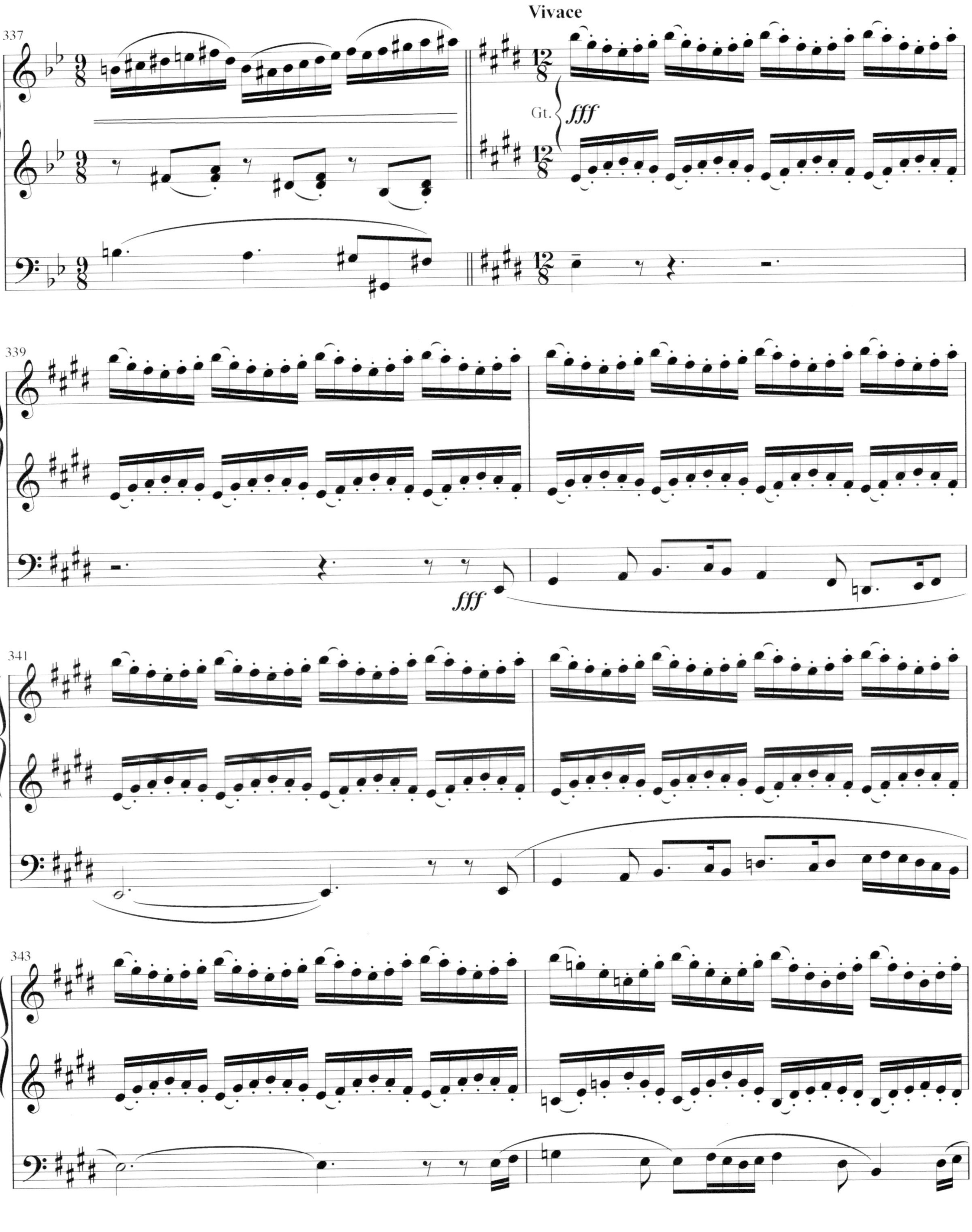

345
Vivace
347
351
353
rit. molto